CELLO

VIDEO GAME MUSIC

Audio arrangements by Peter Deneff

To access audio visit:
www.halleonard.com/mylibrary

5069-0212-1315-2073

ISBN 978-1-5400-3609-4

HAL•LEONARD®

Visit Hal Leonard Online at
www.halleonard.com

Contact us:
Hal Leonard
7777 West Bluemound Road
Milwaukee, WI 53213
Email: info@halleonard.com

In Europe, contact:
Hal Leonard Europe Limited
42 Wigmore Street
Marylebone, London, W1U 2RN
Email: info@halleonardeurope.com

In Australia, contact:
Hal Leonard Australia Pty. Ltd.
4 Lentara Court
Cheltenham, Victoria, 3192 Australia
Email: info@halleonard.com.au

ANGRY BIRDS
Theme

CELLO

By ARI PULKKINEN

To Coda

D.S. al Coda

CODA

ASSASSIN'S CREED III
Main Title

CELLO

By LORNE BALFE

ASSASSIN'S CREED REVELATIONS
Theme

CELLO

By LORNE BALFE

BATTLEFIELD 1942
Theme

CELLO

By JOEL ERIKSSON

CIVILIZATION IV
Baba Yetu

CELLO

Words and Music by
CHRISTOPHER TIN

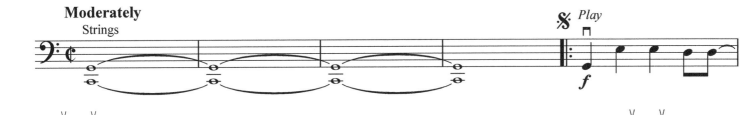

DELTARUNE™
Don't Forget

CELLO

Words and Music by
TOBY FOX

ELDER SCROLLS IV: OBLIVION
Main Theme

CELLO

By JEREMY SOULE

ELDER SCROLLS V: SKYRIM
Dragonborn Theme

CELLO

By JEREMY SOULE

FALLOUT® 4
Theme

CELLO

Composed by INON ZUR

FINAL FANTASY VII
Main Theme

CELLO

By NOBUO UEMATSU

FULL METAL ALCHEMIST
Bratja (Brothers)

CELLO

Words and Music by MICHIRU OSHIMA,
SEIJI MIZUSHIMA and TATIANA NAUMOVA

In a slow 1

IL-2 STURMOVIK: BIRDS OF PREY
Main Theme

Cello

By JEREMY SOULE

SPLINTER CELL: CONVICTION

Cello

Words and Music by KAVEH COHEN
and MICHAEL NIELSEN

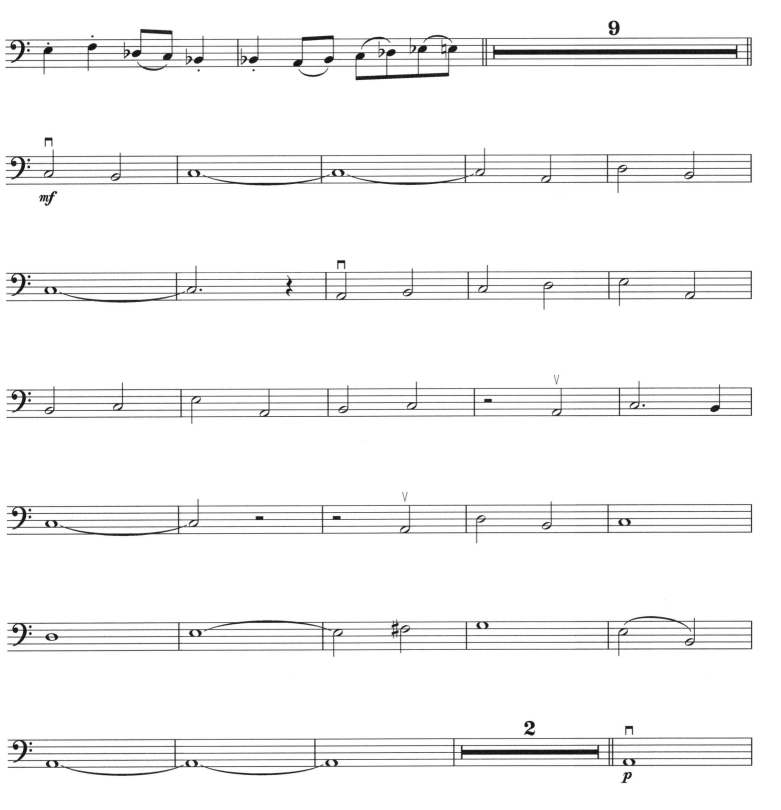

UNDERTALE®
Megalovania

CELLO

Music by TOBY FOX

HAL•LEONARD INSTRUMENTAL PLAY-ALONG

Your favorite songs are arranged just for solo instrumentalists with this outstanding series. Each book includes great full-accompaniment play-along audio so you can sound just like a pro!

Check out halleonard.com for songlists and more titles!

12 Pop Hits
12 songs
00261790	Flute	00261795	Horn
00261791	Clarinet	00261796	Trombone
00261792	Alto Sax	00261797	Violin
00261793	Tenor Sax	00261798	Viola
00261794	Trumpet	00261799	Cello

The Very Best of Bach
15 selections
00225371	Flute	00225376	Horn
00225372	Clarinet	00225377	Trombone
00225373	Alto Sax	00225378	Violin
00225374	Tenor Sax	00225379	Viola
00225375	Trumpet	00225380	Cello

The Beatles
15 songs
00225330	Flute	00225335	Horn
00225331	Clarinet	00225336	Trombone
00225332	Alto Sax	00225337	Violin
00225333	Tenor Sax	00225338	Viola
00225334	Trumpet	00225339	Cello

Chart Hits
12 songs
00146207	Flute	00146212	Horn
00146208	Clarinet	00146213	Trombone
00146209	Alto Sax	00146214	Violin
00146210	Tenor Sax	00146211	Trumpet
00146216	Cello		

Christmas Songs
12 songs
00146855	Flute	00146863	Horn
00146858	Clarinet	00146864	Trombone
00146859	Alto Sax	00146866	Violin
00146860	Tenor Sax	00146867	Viola
00146862	Trumpet	00146868	Cello

Contemporary Broadway
15 songs
00298704	Flute	00298709	Horn
00298705	Clarinet	00298710	Trombone
00298706	Alto Sax	00298711	Violin
00298707	Tenor Sax	00298712	Viola
00298708	Trumpet	00298713	Cello

Disney Movie Hits
12 songs
00841420	Flute	00841424	Horn
00841687	Oboe	00841425	Trombone
00841421	Clarinet	00841426	Violin
00841422	Alto Sax	00841427	Viola
00841686	Tenor Sax	00841428	Cello
00841423	Trumpet		

Disney Solos
12 songs
00841404	Flute	00841506	Oboe
00841406	Alto Sax	00841409	Trumpet
00841407	Horn	00841410	Violin
00841411	Viola	00841412	Cello
00841405	Clarinet/Tenor Sax		
00841408	Trombone/Baritone		
00841553	Mallet Percussion		

Dixieland Favorites
15 songs
00268756	Flute	0068759	Trumpet
00268757	Clarinet	00268760	Trombone
00268758	Alto Sax		

Billie Eilish
9 songs
00345648	Flute	00345653	Horn
00345649	Clarinet	00345654	Trombone
00345650	Alto Sax	00345655	Violin
00345651	Tenor Sax	00345656	Viola
00345652	Trumpet	00345657	Cello

Favorite Movie Themes
13 songs
00841166	Flute	00841168	Trumpet
00841167	Clarinet	00841170	Trombone
00841169	Alto Sax	00841296	Violin

Gospel Hymns
15 songs
00194648	Flute	00194654	Trombone
00194649	Clarinet	00194655	Violin
00194650	Alto Sax	00194656	Viola
00194651	Tenor Sax	00194657	Cello
00194652	Trumpet		

Great Classical Themes
15 songs
00292727	Flute	00292733	Horn
00292728	Clarinet	00292735	Trombone
00292729	Alto Sax	00292736	Violin
00292730	Tenor Sax	00292737	Viola
00292732	Trumpet	00292738	Cello

The Greatest Showman
8 songs
00277389	Flute	00277394	Horn
00277390	Clarinet	00277395	Trombone
00277391	Alto Sax	00277396	Violin
00277392	Tenor Sax	00277397	Viola
00277393	Trumpet	00277398	Cello

Irish Favorites
31 songs
00842489	Flute	00842495	Trombone
00842490	Clarinet	00842496	Violin
00842491	Alto Sax	00842497	Viola
00842493	Trumpet	00842498	Cello
00842494	Horn		

Michael Jackson
11 songs
00119495	Flute	00119499	Trumpet
00119496	Clarinet	00119501	Trombone
00119497	Alto Sax	00119503	Violin
00119498	Tenor Sax	00119502	Accomp.

Jazz & Blues
14 songs
00841438	Flute	00841441	Trumpet
00841439	Clarinet	00841443	Trombone
00841440	Alto Sax	00841444	Violin
00841442	Tenor Sax		

Jazz Classics
12 songs
00151812	Flute	00151816	Trumpet
00151813	Clarinet	00151818	Trombone
00151814	Alto Sax	00151819	Violin
00151815	Tenor Sax	00151821	Cello

Les Misérables
13 songs
00842292	Flute	00842297	Horn
00842293	Clarinet	00842298	Trombone
00842294	Alto Sax	00842299	Violin
00842295	Tenor Sax	00842300	Viola
00842296	Trumpet	00842301	Cello

Metallica
12 songs
02501327	Flute	02502454	Horn
02501339	Clarinet	02501329	Trombone
02501332	Alto Sax	02501334	Violin
02501333	Tenor Sax	02501335	Viola
02501330	Trumpet	02501338	Cello

Motown Classics
15 songs
00842572	Flute	00842576	Trumpet
00842573	Clarinet	00842578	Trombone
00842574	Alto Sax	00842579	Violin
00842575	Tenor Sax		

Pirates of the Caribbean
16 songs
00842183	Flute	00842188	Horn
00842184	Clarinet	00842189	Trombone
00842185	Alto Sax	00842190	Violin
00842186	Tenor Sax	00842191	Viola
00842187	Trumpet	00842192	Cello

Queen
17 songs
00285402	Flute	00285407	Horn
00285403	Clarinet	00285408	Trombone
00285404	Alto Sax	00285409	Violin
00285405	Tenor Sax	00285410	Viola
00285406	Trumpet	00285411	Cello

Simple Songs
14 songs
00249081	Flute	00249087	Horn
00249093	Oboe	00249089	Trombone
00249082	Clarinet	00249090	Violin
00249083	Alto Sax	00249091	Viola
00249084	Tenor Sax	00249092	Cello
00249086	Trumpet	00249094	Mallets

Superhero Themes
14 songs
00363195	Flute	00363200	Horn
00363196	Clarinet	00363201	Trombone
00363197	Alto Sax	00363202	Violin
00363198	Tenor Sax	00363203	Viola
00363199	Trumpet	00363204	Cello

Star Wars
16 songs
00350900	Flute	00350907	Horn
00350913	Oboe	00350908	Trombone
00350903	Clarinet	00350909	Violin
00350904	Alto Sax	00350910	Viola
00350905	Tenor Sax	00350911	Cello
00350906	Trumpet	00350914	Mallet

Taylor Swift
15 songs
00842532	Flute	00842537	Horn
00842533	Clarinet	00842538	Trombone
00842534	Alto Sax	00842539	Violin
00842535	Tenor Sax	00842540	Viola
00842536	Trumpet	00842541	Cello

Video Game Music
13 songs
00283877	Flute	00283883	Horn
00283878	Clarinet	00283884	Trombone
00283879	Alto Sax	00283885	Violin
00283880	Tenor Sax	00283886	Viola
00283882	Trumpet	00283887	Cello

Wicked
13 songs
00842236	Flute	00842241	Horn
00842237	Clarinet	00842242	Trombone
00842238	Alto Sax	00842243	Violin
00842239	Tenor Sax	00842244	Viola
00842240	Trumpet	00842245	Cello

HAL•LEONARD®

101 SONGS

BIG COLLECTIONS OF FAVORITE SONGS ARRANGED FOR SOLO INSTRUMENTALISTS.

101 BROADWAY SONGS

00154199 Flute	$15.99
00154200 Clarinet	$15.99
00154201 Alto Sax	$15.99
00154202 Tenor Sax	$16.99
00154203 Trumpet	$15.99
00154204 Horn	$15.99
00154205 Trombone	$15.99
00154206 Violin	$15.99
00154207 Viola	$15.99
00154208 Cello	$15.99

101 DISNEY SONGS

00244104 Flute	$17.99
00244106 Clarinet	$17.99
00244107 Alto Sax	$17.99
00244108 Tenor Sax	$17.99
00244109 Trumpet	$17.99
00244112 Horn	$17.99
00244120 Trombone	$17.99
00244121 Violin	$17.99
00244125 Viola	$17.99
00244126 Cello	$17.99

101 MOVIE HITS

00158087 Flute	$15.99
00158088 Clarinet	$15.99
00158089 Alto Sax	$15.99
00158090 Tenor Sax	$15.99
00158091 Trumpet	$15.99
00158092 Horn	$15.99
00158093 Trombone	$15.99
00158094 Violin	$15.99
00158095 Viola	$15.99
00158096 Cello	$15.99

101 CHRISTMAS SONGS

00278637 Flute	$15.99
00278638 Clarinet	$15.99
00278639 Alto Sax	$15.99
00278640 Tenor Sax	$15.99
00278641 Trumpet	$15.99
00278642 Horn	$14.99
00278643 Trombone	$15.99
00278644 Violin	$15.99
00278645 Viola	$15.99
00278646 Cello	$15.99

101 HIT SONGS

00194561 Flute	$17.99
00197182 Clarinet	$17.99
00197183 Alto Sax	$17.99
00197184 Tenor Sax	$17.99
00197185 Trumpet	$17.99
00197186 Horn	$17.99
00197187 Trombone	$17.99
00197188 Violin	$17.99
00197189 Viola	$17.99
00197190 Cello	$17.99

101 POPULAR SONGS

00224722 Flute	$17.99
00224723 Clarinet	$17.99
00224724 Alto Sax	$17.99
00224725 Tenor Sax	$17.99
00224726 Trumpet	$17.99
00224727 Horn	$17.99
00224728 Trombone	$17.99
00224729 Violin	$17.99
00224730 Viola	$17.99
00224731 Cello	$17.99

101 CLASSICAL THEMES

00155315 Flute	$15.99
00155317 Clarinet	$15.99
00155318 Alto Sax	$15.99
00155319 Tenor Sax	$15.99
00155320 Trumpet	$15.99
00155321 Horn	$15.99
00155322 Trombone	$15.99
00155323 Violin	$15.99
00155324 Viola	$15.99
00155325 Cello	$15.99

101 JAZZ SONGS

00146363 Flute	$15.99
00146364 Clarinet	$15.99
00146366 Alto Sax	$15.99
00146367 Tenor Sax	$15.99
00146368 Trumpet	$15.99
00146369 Horn	$14.99
00146370 Trombone	$15.99
00146371 Violin	$15.99
00146372 Viola	$15.99
00146373 Cello	$15.99

101 MOST BEAUTIFUL SONGS

00291023 Flute	$16.99
00291041 Clarinet	$16.99
00291042 Alto Sax	$17.99
00291043 Tenor Sax	$17.99
00291044 Trumpet	$16.99
00291045 Horn	$16.99
00291046 Trombone	$16.99
00291047 Violin	$16.99
00291048 Viola	$16.99
00291049 Cello	$17.99

See complete song lists and sample pages at www.halleonard.com

HAL•LEONARD®
www.halleonard.com

Prices, contents and availability subject to change without notice.